triveni

Celebrating 35 Years of
Penguin Random House India

ALSO BY GULZAR

Selected Poems, translated by Pavan K. Verma
Suspected Poems, translated by Pavan K. Verma
Green Poems, translated by Pavan K. Verma
Yudhisthir & Draupadi, translated by Pavan K. Verma

100 Lyrics, translated by Sunjoy Shekhar
Another 100 Lyrics, translated by Sunjoy Shekhar
Half a Rupee Stories, translated by Sunjoy Shekhar

Actually . . . I Met Them, translated by Maharghya Chakraborty

FORTHCOMING—FALL OF 2024

Caged In, translated by Sathya Saran

triveni

GULZAR

Translated by NEHA R. KRISHNA

PENGUIN

An imprint of Penguin Random House

HAMISH HAMILTON

USA | Canada | UK | Ireland | Australia
New Zealand | India | South Africa | China | Singapore

Hamish Hamilton is part of the Penguin Random House group of companies
whose addresses can be found at global.penguinrandomhouse.com

Published by Penguin Random House India Pvt. Ltd
4th Floor, Capital Tower 1, MG Road,
Gurugram 122 002, Haryana, India

First published in Hamish Hamilton by Penguin Random House India 2023

ISBN 9780670098224

Typeset in RequiemText by Manipal Digital Systems, Manipal
Printed at Manipal Technologies Limited, Manipal

www.penguin.co.in

For Yaseen Anwer

Triveni

I was rowing in words and meters of poetry when I happened to invent the form of Triveni. It's a short poem of three lines. The first two lines make a complete thought, like a couplet of a ghazal. But the third line adds an extra dimension, which is hidden or out of sight in the first two lines.

Triveni ends revealing the hidden thought, which changes the perspective or extends the thought of the couplet.

The name Triveni refers to the confluence of three distinct streams or rivers at Prayag. The deep-green waters of Jamuna meet the golden Ganga, and hidden from view is the mythical Sarswati, flowing quietly beneath.

'Triveni' is to reveal 'Saraswati', poetically.

देर तक आस्माँ पे उड़ते रहे
इक परिन्दे के बाल-व-पर सारे

बाज़ अपना शिकार ले के गया !

All the fur and feathers of a bird
Kept flying in the sky for a long time

The falcon swooped away with its prey!

Neha, a young competent poet, was rowing in Triveni. She wished to translate Triveni into a Japanese form of poetry called Tanka. I felt inquisitive.

She has explained it in her translator's note.

I hope you too feel as inquisitive while reading it.

I found it very interesting.

Gulzar

Translator's Note

Tanka is a short lyric poem. Various poetic elements, like mood, theme, nature, characters, etc., are posed in a particular structure that give Tanka its body and soul. With this concept note, I am addressing the fundamental techniques of writing a Tanka. It will also assist readers to comprehend and appreciate the structure.

What Is Tanka?

Tanka is a lyrical poem, a short verse, a short song. It is one of the oldest forms, originating in Japan in the seventh century. A traditional Japanese Tanka has thirty-one morae or sounds that follow a 5-7-5-7-7 sound structure.

The Difference between Traditional Tanka and Contemporary Tanka

Tanka in contemporary English is more flexible and does not adhere to the traditional 5-7-5-7-7 syllabic structure or the pattern of short/long/short/long/long line format.

Why Transcreate Triveni into Tanka?

The aesthetic sense, the grace of cadence and the rich imagery of Tanka appear inclined to Triveni. Even in Triveni, images are juxtaposed with the technique of link and shift. Just like any lyrical Tanka poem, Triveni can also be composed and sung. The length of images of Triveni fits well in Tanka, as it gives more space to retain the multilayered essence. Triveni's L3 strongly adds to or changes the narration of L1 and L2. In the same way, Tanka has a very strong and unexpected L5.

There is musicality in these short poems, even though they never rhyme, which allows them to be enriched with a rustic edge, conjuring up a magical and musical image.

Methods of Writing Tanka

There are many ways of writing Tanka. The 2/3, 3/2, 4/1 and 1/4 are the ratio of the lines for arranging the two images in that structure. There is one-sentence Tanka structured in five lines. Then there is three-image Tanka. One of the popular methods is Tanka with a pivot.

The 2/3 or 3/2 image format: L1 and L2 together make the first image and the second image runs from L3 to L5 and vice versa.

2/3 Image format

साँवले साहिल पे गुलमोहर का पेड़
जैसे लैला की माँग में सिन्दूर

धरम बदल गया बेचारी का

a gulmohar tree
at dusk—
as Laila wears vermilion
    her religion
      allegedly changes

3/2 Image format

कोई चादर की तरह खींचे चला जाता है दरिया
कौन सोया है तले इस के जिसे ढूँढ रहे हैं!

डूबने वाले को भी चैन से सोने नहीं देते!

like a sheet of cloth
they pull the river to search
who sleeps underneath
    the one who drowned
cannot even rest in peace

4/1 or 1/4 image format: First image runs from L1 to L4 and L5
is the second image and vice versa.

4/1 Image Format

रात के पेड़ पे कल ही तो उसे देखा था
चाँद बस गिरने ही वाला था फ़लक से, पक कर

सूरज आया था, ज़रा उसकी तलाशी लेना

on the night tree
had seen yesterday
a ripe moon

was about to fall—
frisk the sun, it had come

Pivot: Often word(s) or a phrase is employed at line three in Tanka in such a way that it reflects in both the images. The transition is so smooth, hence L3 can be read as a part of the upper verse and as a part of the lower verse.

यह आधा चाँद काले आसमाँ ऊपर
अंधेरा चाटती है, जीभ से जब रात,

कढ़ाई सुबह तक चट कर के जाती है!

this half-moon
above in the black sky
till morning
the night licks with its tongue
darkness from the wok

The above poem has two images hinged with a pivot, that can be read as follows,

this half moon
above in the black sky
till morning

till morning
the night licks with its tongue
darkness from the wok

Line 3: 'Till morning' is a 'pivot' in this poem. It can be read with the upper verse and the lower verse.

One-sentence Tanka: Single image/thought runs from L1 to L5; sometimes there are two images put together with a conjunction. The poem below can be read in one breath because of *as* in L3.

सारी वादी उदास बैठी है,
मौसम-ए-गुल ने ख़ुदकुशी कर ली।

'माइन्ज़' पर पाव रख दिया उसने।

in despair
the whole valley crouches
as spring
pledged suicide
stepping on mines

Three-image Tanka: Three images are put together in this Tanka—from L1 to L2 is one image, from L3 to L4 is the second image, and L5 is the third image.

तेरी सूरत जो भरी रहती हैं आँखों में हमेशा
अजनबी लोग भी पहचाने से लगते हैं मुझे

तेरे रिश्ते में तो दुनिया ही पिरो ली मैंने!

your face
always fills the eyes,
strangers too
seem familiar to me—
I knitted a world around you

More about Tanka Aesthetic and How It Incorporates Triveni

Yūgen is all about mystery and depth that root the emotions. When any moment stirs an ineffable feeling, a sudden enlightenment that illuminates your soul and strikes ripples of emotions that cannot be explained to anyone or oneself, that under-the-skin sensation is Yūgen. It is a mysterious evocative tap on your subconscious. Seldom Yūgen refers to a state of mind or a reality, or a blend of both, that lets you experience mystical profundity.

साथ ही साथ चला आया है, जितना भी सफ़र है
रास्ते पैरों में रस्सियों की तरह लिपटे हुए हैं

लौट के जाने से बल खुलते नहीं, और चढ़ेंगे।

have come along
as much as the journey was . . .
roads envelop legs like ropes
grip tightens on return
rather than loosening

The above poem evokes Yūgen, a sensation of life. The roads that wrap the legs like ropes are memories that you cannot let go of.

Wabi-Sabi is one of the core aesthetics of Japanese culture that also reflects in their literature and art. A philosophy that emphasizes conceiving a deeper connection with nature and primarily having harmony with your truest inner self. It artfully stirs the mind to constantly value the beauty of imperfections of routine life and accept the cycle of life. It is a way of life encapsulating the beauty of simplicity, fragile life, flaws, and the art of appreciating the touch of time and fragility.

Wabi is about recognizing the beauty in serene and modest expression while incorporating rustic grace and quietude. It bids manifestation of detachment from the concept of flawlessness and material perfection.

Sabi suggests that beauty lies between the lines of what is in sight, an unknown space underlining the hidden meaning of everything. It is the gentle touch of the passing of time in which everything fades graciously and embraces the silhouette of ageing, decaying, loneliness, melancholy, sorrow and stillness.

चौधवें चाँद को फिर आग लगी है देखो
फिर बहुत देर तलक आज उजाला होगा

राख हो जायेगा जब फिर से अमावस होगी!

full moon burns
its whiteness will linger
one more time
when it turns to ashes
        —*Amāvásyā*

The aesthetic of Wabi-Sabi reflects in this poem. We all are enchanted by the beauty of the full moon. Wabi enriches the rustic light of the cratered moon. Sabi helps us to enjoy the depth of the darkness of the Amāvásyā.

Link and shift is a technique that pledges a movement between the images. Linking is a connection between the contrasts of juxtaposed images, whereas shifting advocates the transitioning of one image to another. The imagistic tempo of link and shift allows a deeper dimension of meaning to emerge and enrich the context.

बस हवा ही भर रही है गोलों में
सूइ चुभ जाए तो पिचक जायें

लोग गुस्से में बम नहीं बनते।

if needle jabs
mere air-filled balls
will deflate—
in fury
people don't become bombs

With the help of the link and shift technique, the two images are put together in contrast to each other. The image from L1 to L3 shows air-filled balls can be deflated by a needle prick. Just like people who tick like bombs in anger but don't blast, just silently sit with puffed cheeks displaying anger, as put in L4 and L5.

What Is Tanka Doha?

Tanka Doha was introduced by Kala Ramesh, one of my mentors. It is inspired by Kabir's doha, a fifteenth-century Indian mystic–poet–saint, and is a couplet of twenty-four sound units. In the same way, two Tanka with their haikai spirits are paired together to tell a story. This form of twin Tanka allows stories to brew in a short span of ten lines. The link and shift and the white space between the two Tanka retain the spirit of Triveni in the form of Tanka Doha.

पत्थर की दीवार पे, लकड़ी के इक फ्रेम में, काँच के अन्दर फूल बने हैं
एक तसव्वुर ख़ुशबू का और कितने सारे पहनावों में बन्द किया है

इश्क़ पे दिल का एक लिबास ही काफ़ी था, अब कितनी पोशाकें पहनेगा?

on the stone wall
flowers drawn inside a glass
are framed in wood . . .
sealed under countless layers
this fancy of fragrance

> *of heart*
> *one attire was enough*
> *on love*
> *how many costumes*
> *does it intend to wear*

An exquisite example of Tanka Doha, the above poem has the element of link and shift that allows the story to flow smoothly.

Punctuations

In English, Tanka or Haiku, the verse or the sentence, never starts with capital letter and never ends with a full stop. Punctuation marks other than full stop and sometimes blank spaces or indentation are used to add deliberate pauses in the poem. But it cannot be overdone, as Tanka and Haiku breathe the aesthetics of simplicity.

Following are a couple of poems as examples:

Poem 1:

ऐसे बिखरे हैं रात दिन, जैसे
मोतियों वाला हार टूट गया

तुमने मुझे पिरो के रखा था

days and nights
like a broken string of pearls
have scattered
it was you
who kept me threaded

No punctuation or indentation is used in this poem. Still, two images that run from L1 to L3 and from L4 to L5 can be read.

We can use em dash to add a deliberate pause at the end of L3.

days and nights
like a broken string of pearls
have scattered—
it was you
who kept me threaded

We can use indentation to add a deliberate pause before L4 begins.

days and nights
like a broken string of pearls
have scattered
        it was you
who kept me threaded

* * *

Poem 2:

कोई चादर की तरह खींचे चला जाता है दरिया
कौन सोया है तले इस के जिसे ढूँढ रहे हैं!

डूबने वाले को भी चैन से सोने नहीं देते!

like a sheet of cloth
they pull the river to search
who sleeps underneath
the one who drowned
cannot even rest in peace

Here is another poem with no punctuation or indentation. 3/2 image format can be read here. The first image that runs from L1 to L3 and the second image that runs from L4 to L5.

Using Ellipsis:

like a sheet of cloth
they pull the river to search
who sleeps underneath . . .
the one who drowned
cannot even rest in peace

Using Indentation:

like a sheet of cloth
they pull the river to search
who sleeps underneath
     the one who drowned
   cannot even rest in peace

Lastly, I would say—feel the pauses and enjoy the emotions and feelings which inhabit these beautiful Tanka.

Triveni

उड़ के जाते हुए पंछी ने बस इतना देखा
देर तक हाथ हिलाती रही वह शाख़ फ़िज़ा में

अलविदा कहती थी या पास बुलाती थी उसे?

bird leaves
while the branch sways
in the wind—
urging it to come back
or bidding a goodbye?

क्या पता, कब कहाँ से मारेगी
बस की मैं ज़िन्दगी से डरता हूँ

मौत का क्या है, एक बार मारेगी

who knows
where and when it will strike,
just life I fear—
as death
can only kill once

सब पे आती है, सब की बारी है
मौत मुनसिफ़ है, कम-ओ-बेश नहीं

ज़िन्दगी सब पे क्यों नहीं आती?

to all it comes
everyone has their turn,
death is just
neither less nor more—
why doesn't life happen to all?

भीगा भीगा सा क्यों है ये अख़बार
अपने हॉकर को कल से चेंज करो

पाँच सौ गाँव बह गये इस साल!

this newspaper
is soaked through, why?
from tomorrow
switch your hawker . . .
'500 villages swept away this year!'

चौधवें चाँद को फिर आग लगी है देखो
फिर बहुत देर तलक आज उजाला होगा

राख हो जायेगा जब फिर से अमावस होगी!

full moon burns
its whiteness will linger
one more time
   when it turns to ashes
          —Amāvásyā

रात के पेड़ पे कल ही तो उसे देखा था
चाँद बस गिरने ही वाला था फ़लक से, पक कर

सूरज आया था, ज़रा उसकी तलाशी लेना

yesterday
had seen on the night tree
a ripe moon
was about to fall—
frisk the sun, it had come

जुल्फ़ में यूँ चमक रही है बूँद
जैसे बेरी में तनहा एक जुगनू

क्या बुरा है जो छत टपकती है

the drop
on the hair shines
like lone firefly
among the berries . . .
what's bad if the roof leaks?

शाम से शम्मा जली देख रही है रस्ता
कोई परवाना इधर आया नहीं, देर हुई!

सौत होगी मेरी, जो पास में जलती होगी!

since evening
a burning candle awaits
yet no moth came
it's late—flickering nearby
    must be his second wife

इतने लोगो में, कह दो आँखों से
इतना ऊँचा न ऐसे बोला करें

सब मेरा नाम जान जाते हैं

ask your eyes
to not be this loud
in public . . .
                    everyone
gets to know my name

साँवले साहिल पे गुलमोहर का पेड़
जैसे लैला की माँग में सिन्दूर

धरम बदल गया बेचारी का

a gulmohar tree
at dusk—
as Laila wears vermilion
her religion
allegedly changes

बस हवा ही भर रही है गोलों में
सूइ चुभ जाए तो पिचक जायें

लोग गुस्से में बम नहीं बनते।

if needle jabs
mere air-filled balls
will deflate—
in fury
people don't become bombs

सारा दिन बैठा मैं, हाथ में लेकर ख़ाली कासा
रात जो गुज़री, चाँद की कौड़ी डाल गई उसमें

सूद ख़ोर सूरज मुझ से यह भी ले जाएगा!

all day I sit
with empty begging bowl,
passing night puts in
a Moon Cowrie—
usurious sun will take this too

आओ, सारे पहन लें आइने
सारे देखेंगे अपना ही चेहरा

सबको, सारे हसीं लगेंगे यहाँ!

let us all
wear mirrors, all will see
their own faces
all will look charming
to everyone here

हाथ मिला कर देखा, और कुछ सोच के मेरा नाम लिया
जैसे ये सरवरक़ किसी नॉवल पर पहले देखा है

रिश्ते कुछ बस बंद किताबों में ही अच्छे लगते हैं।

eyeing me thoughtfully
shook hands, called my name
as if seen this novel cover before—
relationships: only some
look good inside closed books

दूसरी जंगे आलम को तो बंद हुए भी बीते साल
अब भी कुछ जापानी अफ़सर, छुपे मिले हैं डयूटी पर

तुमसे अब कब मिलना होगा? या अब भी नाराज़ हो तुम?

some Japanese soldiers
in hiding are discovered
years after World War II—
when can we meet?
or are you still upset?

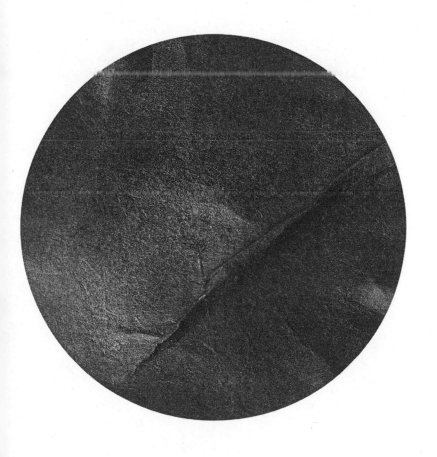

न हर सहर का वो झगड़ा, न शब की बेचैनी
न चूल्हा जलता है घर में, न आँखे जलती है

मैं कितने अमन से घर में उदास रहता हूँ।

no morning brawl
no restlessness at night
no eyes burn as
no mud-oven's been lit in the house . . .
how placidly sad I live by

सितारे चाँद की कश्ती में रात लाती है
सहर के आने से पहले ही बिक भी जाते है

बहुत ही अच्छा है व्यापार इन दिनों शब का!

fetches stars
on a moon boat and sells
before dawn
       the night does
a great trade these days

सामने आये मेरे, देखा मुझे, बात भी की
मुस्कुराये भी, पुरानी किसी पहचान की ख़ातिर

कल का अख़बार था, बस देख लिया, रख भी दिया।

on seeing
we talked and even smiled
for old times' sake—
with just a glance putting down
a day-old newspaper

शोला सा गुज़रता है मेरे जिस्म से हो कर
किस लौ से उतारा है ख़ुदावंद ने तुम को

तिनकों का मेरा घर है, कभी आओ तो क्या हो?

fire runs through my body,
with what flame did the Lord
carve you?
my house is a stack of straws
what will happen if you come?

रोज़ उठ कर चाँद टांगा है फ़लक पे रात को
रोज़ दिन की रोशनी में रात तक आया किये

हाथ भर के फ़ासले को उम्र भर चलना पड़ा।

arose . . . walked daily
from day to night and hung
the moon in the sky

    for a distance just at hand
    had to trudge all life

कोई चादर की तरह खींचे चला जाता है दरिया
कौन सोया है तले इस के जिसे ढूँढ रहे हैं!

डूबने वाले को भी चैन से सोने नहीं देते!

like a sheet of cloth
they pull the river to search
who sleeps underneath
        the one who drowned
    cannot even rest in peace

बस एक पानी की आवाज़ लपलपाती है
कि घाट छोड़ के माँझी तमाम जा भी चुके

चलो ना! चाँद की कश्ती में झील पार करें।

as all sailors leave
the shore resonates with
splashes of water
  let us cross the lake
  on the moon boat

कुछ इंतज़ार में, कुछ हिज्र, कुछ विसाल में थे
बहुत से लोग थे कल रात चाँद कश्ती में

मगर सहर की किसी को भी आरज़ू ही न थी

some in waiting
some in separation
some in union . . .
last night many were on the moon boat
    yet   no one longed for dawn

काश आये कोई शायर की सुने
शे'र के दर्द से मर जायेगा यह

चाँदनी फाँक रहा था शब भर!

wishing . . . someone
to come listen to the poet
he will die
from the pain of a couplet—
all night was grazing moonlight

इक निवाले सी निगल जाती है ये नींद मुझे
रेशमी मोज़े निगल जाते हैं पाँव जैसे

सुबह लगता है कि ताबूत से निकला हूँ अभी।

sleep swallows me
like a morsel
as silk socks swallow feet . . .
in the morning it feels
out of the coffin I rise

उम्र के खेल में इक तरफ़ा है ये रस्साकशी
इक सिरा मुझको दिया होता तो इक बात भी थी।

मुझसे तगड़ा भी है और सामने आता भी नहीं।

this biased tug of war
of life would be a thing
if I had one end
to hold—stronger than me
yet doesn't face me

ख़फ़ा रहे वह हमेशा तो कुछ नहीं होता
कभी कभी जो मिले आँखें फूट पड़ती हैं

बताएँ किस को बहारों में दर्द होता है।

her displeasure, never
disturbed me, yet on seldom meet
the eyes brim—
to whom shall I tell
it aches in the springs

आपकी ख़ातिर अगर हम लूट भी लें आसमाँ
क्या मिलेगा चंद चमकीले से शीशे तोड़ कर?

चाँद चुभ जायेगा उँगली में तो ख़ून आ जायेगा।

even if I steal
the sky for you
what will you gain
by plucking some bright glasses—
finger pricked by the moon will bleed

लोग मेलों में भी गुम हो कर मिले हैं बारहा
दास्तानों के किसी दिलचस्प से इक मोड़ पर

यूँ हमेशा के लिये भी क्या बिछड़ता है कोई!

people lost
even in melas often meet
in stories
at some interesting turn—
does someone part forever?

रात, परेशां सड़कों पर इक डोलता साया
खम्बे से टकरा के गिरा और फ़ौत हुआ

अंधेरे की नाजायज़ औलाद थी कोई!

a wiggly shadow
upset on the street at night
hits a pole, falls and dies—
           must be an illicit
    offspring of the darkness

इस से पहले रात मेरे घर छापा मारे
मैं तनहाई ताले में बंद कर आता हूँ

'गरबा' नाचता हूँ फिर घूमती सड़कों पर!

afore the night
reaves my house
I lock loneliness in
then on swirling streets
dance garba

तमाम सफ़्हे किताबों के फड़फड़ाने लगे
हवा धकेल के दरवाज़ा आ गयी घर में

कभी हवा की तरह तुम भी आया जाया करो!

books' pages rustle
when wind barges
into the house
you too, like the wind
come and go, sometimes

पौ फूटी है और किरनों से काँच बजे हैं
घर जाने का वक़्त हुआ है, पाँच बजे हैं

सारी शब घड़ियाल ने चौकीदारी की है!

dawn breaks
and glass tinkles at the touch
of sunlight . . .
the clock has guarded all night
five it is, time to be home

बेलगाम उड़ती हैं कुछ ख़्वाहिशें ऐसे दिल में
'मेक्सिकन' फ़िल्मों में कुछ दौड़ते घोड़े जैसे।

थान पर बाँधी नहीं जातीं सभी ख़्वाहिशें मुझसे।

in heart
some desires fly unbridled
like horses running
in Mexican films—desires
all can't be tied

कभी कभी बाज़ार में यूँ भी हो जाता है
कीमत ठीक थी, जेब में इतने दाम नहीं थे

ऐसे ही इक बार मैं, तुमको हार आया था।

happens sometimes,
things were priced fairly
in the market but
money in the pocket wasn't enough—
just the way I lost you once

न हम मुड़े, न कहीं रास्ता मुड़ा अपना
नशेब आये कहीं, और कहीं फ़राज़ आये!

मैं नीचे नीचे चला, तुम बुलंदियों पे रहीं!

we took no turn
nor did the road, but there were
highs and lows—
you chose the height
I savoured the ground

वह मेरे साथ ही था दूर तक मगर इक दिन
जो मुड़ के देखा तो वह और मेरे साथ न था

फटी हो जेब तो कुछ सिक्के खो भी जाते हैं।

till far
he was with me but not when
I turned back one day—
      some coins go missing
    if the pocket has a hole

वह जिससे साँस का रिश्ता बंधा हुआ था मेरा
दबा के दाँत तले साँस काट दी उसने

कटी पतंग का मांझा मुहल्ले भर में लुटा!

the one with whom
the bond of my breath was tied,
snipped it with the teeth
            everyone in the streets
grabbed this string of torn kite

कुछ मेरे यार थे, रहते थे मेरे साथ हमेशा
कोई आया था, उन्हें लेके गया, फिर नहीं लौटे

शेल्फ़ से निकली किताबों की जगह ख़ाली पड़ी है।

a few friends
living with me, left with someone
and never returned—
on the shelf there're empty spaces
from where books were removed

इतनी लम्बी अंगड़ाई ली लड़की ने
शोले जैसे सूरज पर जा हाथ लगा

छाले जैसा चाँद पड़ा है उंगली पर!

it blazed when
yawning stretch of a girl's hands
touched the sun—
a moon-shaped blister
is on the finger

बुड़ बुड़ करते लफ़्जों को चिमटी से पकड़ो
फेंको और मसल दो पैर की एड़ी से।

अफवाहों को ख़ूँ पीने की आदत है।

with a pair of tongs
seize the burbling words,
fling them,
crush them with heels—
    rumours are bloodsuckers

परिचयाँ बँट रही हैं गलियों में
अपने कातिल का इन्तख़ाब करो

वक़्त यह सख़्त चुनाव का।

in the streets
slips are being handed out
Choose Your Killer—
stern it is,
the time of election

कुछ ऐसी एहतियात से निकला है चाँद फिर
जैसे अंधेरी रात में खिड़की पे आओ तुम।

क्या चाँद और ज़मीं में भी कोई खिंचाव है?

with such care the moon rises
like you come to the window
on a dark night—
          is there an attraction
between the moon and earth too?

ज़मीन घूमती है गिर्द आफ़ताब के
ज़मी के गिर्द चाँद घूमता है रात दिन

हैं तीन हम, हमारी फेमिली है तीन की।

earth circles the sun
moon goes round the earth
night and day—
just we,
our family of three

चूड़ी के टुकड़े थे, पैर में चुभते ही ख़ूँ बह निकला
नंगे पाँव खेल रहा था, लड़का अपने आँगन में

बाप ने कल फिर दारू पीके माँ की बाँह मरोड़ी थी।

broken bangles in the yard
when pricked the foot, blood oozed
boy was playing barefoot—
yesterday, his drunkard father
twisted his mother's wrist . . . again

कुछ आफ़ताब और उड़े कायनात में
मैं आसमान की जटायें खोल रहा था

वह तौलिये से गीले बाल छाँट रही थीं।

some rays of sun
scatter in the universe,
I untangle
the dreadlocks of the sky . . .
she flicks wet hair with a towel

जंगल से गुज़रते थे तो कभी बस्ती भी कहीं मिल जाती थी
अब बस्ती में कोई पेड़ नज़र आ जाये तो जी भर आता है

दीवार पे सब्ज़ा देखके अब याद आता है, पहले जंगल था।

while crossing the jungle
a hamlet sometimes appeared . . .
heart now brims to see a tree,
green grass on the wall
reminds—there was a jungle

जाते जाते एक बार तो कार की बत्ती सुर्ख़ हुई
शायद तुमने सोचा हो कि रुक जाओ, या लौट आओ

सिग्नल तोड़ के लेकिन तुम इक दूसरी जानिब घूम गये।

car's tail light turned red,
maybe while leaving, you thought
to stop
or to come back—but
breaking the signal, you veered off

इस तेज़ धुप में भी अकेला नहीं था मैं
इक साया मेरे आगे पीछे दौड़ता रहा

तनहा तेरे ख़याल ने रहने नहीं दिया

I wasn't alone
even in this scorching heat
a shadow
raced back and forth—your thought
never let me be lonely

तेरी सूरत जो भरी रहती हैं आँखों में हमेशा
अजनबी लोग भी पहचाने से लगते हैं मुझे

तेरे रिश्ते में तो दुनिया ही पिरो ली मैंने!

your face
always fills the eyes,
strangers too
seem familiar to me—
I knitted a world around you

कोई सूरत भी मुझे पूरी नज़र आती नहीं
आँख के शीशे मेरे चटख़े हुए है

टुकड़ों टुकड़ों में सभी लोग मिले हैं मुझको

even faces
are not visible completely
as the glasses
on my eyes bear cracks—
in pieces I have got everyone

एक से घर हैं सभी, एक से बाशिन्दे हैं
अजनबी शहर में कुछ अजनबी लगता ही नहीं

एक से दर्द हैं सब, एक ही से रिश्ते हैं

houses are same,
natives too—this foreign city
doesn't feel alien
        all pains are alike
      so are the relationships

पेड़ों के कटने से नाराज़ हुए हैं पंछी
दाना चुगने भी नहीं आते मकानों पे परिन्दे

कोई बुलबुल भी नहीं बैठती अब शे'र पे आकर!

irked by cutting of trees
birds don't visit the houses
to peck at grains
even nightingale doesn't come
       to perch on the poem

ज़रा 'पैलेट' सम्भालो रंग-ओ-बू का
मैं कैनवस आसमाँ का खोलता हूँ

बनाओ फिर से सूरत आदमी की।

hold the palette
of colours and fragrance—
I unfurl
the canvas of the sky
draw again 'a man's portrait'

अजीब कपड़ा दिया है मुझे सिलाने को
कि तूल खींचूँ अगर, अरज़ छूट जाता है

उधड़ने सीने ही में उमर कट गई सारी

odd fabric
I have got for sewing
if I pull the length
the width falls short—
lost the life in unstitching-stitching

चाँद के माथे पर बचपन की चोट के दाग़ नज़र आते है
रोड़े, पत्थर और गुलेलों से दिन भर खेला करता था

बहुत कहा, आवारा उल्काओं की संगत ठीक नहीं!

childhood scar
on the moon's forehead . . .
day long played with
slingshots, gravels—warned often
vagrant meteor allies are no good

हवाएँ ज़ख़्मी हो जाती है काँटे-दार तारों से
जबीं घिसता है दरिया जब तेरी सरहद गुज़रता है

मेरा इक यार है 'दरिया-ए-रावी' पार रहता है

barbed wire
scars the winds, rubs forehead
when river crosses
the border—a friend of mine
lives across the Raavi

मैं सब सामान लेकर आ गया इस पार सरहद के
मेरी गरदन किसी ने क़तल कर के उस तरफ़ रख ली

उसे मुझ से बिछड़ जाना गवारा ही न हुआ शायद

while coming
to this side of the border
with my belongings
someone slit my neck—perhaps
to him, parting was unbearable

मैं रहता इस तरफ़ हूँ यार की दीवार के लेकिन
मेरा साया अभी दीवार के उस पार गिरता है।

बड़ी कच्ची सी सरहद एक अपने जिस्म-ओ-जाँ की है।

this side of beloved's wall
I live, yet my shadow falls
on the other side—
such a weak fence
our body and soul possess

जिस से भी पूछा ठिकाना उसका
इक पता और बता जाता है

या वह बेघर है, या हरजाई है

whomever I ask
about his whereabouts
gives a new address
I wonder if he is homeless
or a vagabond

क्या बतलायें? कैसे याद की मौत हुई
डूब के पानी में परछाई फौत हुई

ठहरे पानी भी कितने गहरे होते हैं

can't say
how the memory died . . .
drowning in
the shadow perished—
deep down . . . still waters too run

छू के फ़ानूस गुज़रती है सबा जब घर से
तेरी आवाज़ के छींटे से छिड़क जाती है

गुदगुदाने से तू ऐसे ही हँसा करती है।

fondling chandelier
the breeze when sways through
the house,
it splatters your voice
            on being tickled
            you would laugh alike

इक इक याद उठाओ और पलकों से पोंछ के वापस रख दो
अश्क नहीं ये आँख में रखे कीमती-कीमती शीशे हैं

ताक़ से गिर के क़ीमती चीजें टूट भी जाया करती हैं

one by one
pick the memories
wipe off
from the eyelashes
and keep them back

      settled
      in the eyes are not tears but
      precious glasses—
      falling from the wall recess
      priceless things often break

ऐसे बिखरे हैं रात दिन, जैसे
मोतियों वाला हार टूट गया

तुमने मुझे पिरो के रखा था

days and nights
like a broken string of pearls
have scattered
                it was you
who kept me threaded

ज़िन्दगी क्या है, जानने के लिए
ज़िंदा रहना बहुत ज़रूरी है

आज तक कोई भी रहा तो नहीं

it's important
to stay alive to know
what is life—
       thus far
nobody has ever lived

दरिया जब अपने पानी खंगालते हैं तुग़यानी में
जितना कुछ मिलता है वह सब साहिल पर रख जाते हैं

ले जाते हैं कर्म जो लोगों ने फेंके हों दरिया में!

with force when river
swills its water and puts on shore
all things amassed
      it takes back deeds
people dumped in the river

है नहीं जो दिखाई देता है
आईने पर छपा हुआ चेहरा

तर्जुमा आईने का ठीक नहीं

it's not
what you see—
this face in the mirror
is just a poor translation
it offers

झुग्गी के अंदर एक बच्चा रोते रोते
माँ से रूठ के अपने आप ही सो भी गया है

थोड़ी देर को 'युद्ध विश्राम' हुआ है शायद

irked by mother
a wailing kid falls asleep
on its own
inside the hut—
it's a brief ceasefire, maybe

जिस्म के ख़ोल के अन्दर ढूँड रहा हूँ और कोई
एक जो मैं हूँ, एक जो कोई और चमकता है

एक मयान में दो तलवारें कैसे रहती हैं?

under the skin
I look for somebody else,
one—the way I am
and some other—who shines
how two swords be in one scabbard?

यह सुस्त धूप अभी नीचे भी नहीं उतरी
यह सर्दियों में बहुत देर छत पर सोती है

लिहाफ़ उम्मीद का भी कब से तारतार हुआ

this lazy sunlight
yet to descend the roof,
sleeps for long in winters—
how long since the quilt
of hope too is shredded

ऐसे आई है तेरी याद अचानक
जैसे पगडंडी कोई पेड़ों से निकले।

इक घने माज़ी के जंगल में मिली हो।

sudden arrival
of your memory
like a path through trees
in the deep forest of the past
I find you

लब तेरे 'मीर' ने भी देखे हैं
पंखुड़ी इक गुलाब की सी है

बातें सुनते तो 'ग़ालिब' हो जाते

your lips
like the petals of a rose
even Mir has espied—
hearing you speak
would have made him Ghalib

तेरे शहर पहुंच तो जाता
रस्ते में दरिया पड़ते हैं!

पुल सब तूने जला दिये थे!

I could reach
your city but there are rivers
en route—
　　　all the bridges
　　　you have burned

इतने अर्से बाद हैंगर से कोट निकाला
कितना लम्बा बाल मिला है कॉलर पर

पिछले जाड़ों में पहना था, याद आता है।

took off from a hanger,
the coat collar bears
a long hair strand
    I recall
    wearing it last winter

खिड़कियां बन्द हैं, दरवाज़ों पे भी ताले लगे हैं
कैसे यह ख़्वाब चले आते हैं फिर कमरे के अन्दर?

नींद में कोई तो रोज़न है, खुला रहता है!

doors are locked,
windows are closed, then how
dreams enter the room—
        a vent in sleep
        must be open

तुम्हारे होंठ बहुत ख़ुश्क ख़ुश्क रहते हैं
इन्ही लबों पे कभी ताज़ा शेर मिलते थे

यह तुमने होंठों पे अफ़साने रख लिये कब से?

fresh poetry
used to nestle on your lips
but now so dry
since when you let stories
to settle on them

एक खेत है, इक दरिया है
साथ साथ रहते, बहते हैं।

माही, मज़ारे, सब चाकर हैं।

a river,
a farming land
dwell together
flow together
sailor, tiller, all are servants

मैं बस में बैठा हुआ ढूँढने लगा मुड़ के
न जाने क्यों यह लगा तुम वहीं कहीं पर हो

तुम्हारा सैंट किसी और ने था लगाया हुआ।

sensing you close
I turn around and look
while sitting on the bus
someone is fragrant
    with your scent

कुछ इस तरह ख़याल तेरा जल उठा की बस
जैसे दिया सलाई जली हो अँधेरे में

अब फूँक भी दो वर्ना ये ऊँगली जलाएगा

your thought
strikes a matchstick
in the dark—
blow out the fire
it can burn finger!

काँटे वाली तार पे किसने गीले कपड़े टांगें हैं
ख़ून टपकता रहता है और नाली में बह जाता है

क्यों इस फ़ौजी की बेवा हर रोज़ ये वर्दी धोती है

each day
blood-dripping clothes
on barbed wire—
why a dead soldier's wife
washes his uniform

जला के फूला नहीं समाता जो बस्तिओं को
वह रू-सियाह आसमान को छूने लग गया है

धुएँ के चोले पे ख़ून की बू के दाग़ भी है

feels elated
after burning the villages,
that black-faced
is now touching the sky—
bloodstains on pall of smoke . . . stink

बस दिन ढला कि आले में इक चेहरा जल उठा
इक ताज़ा ज़ख़्म की तरह से रोशनी हुई।

और जलती शमओं से कई क़तरे पिघल गए।

just when the day sets
a face lights up in a wall-niche
like a fresh wound
from the lit candles
many drops melt away

अब तो अदब, हुनर-ओ-फ़न भी बाँट चुके हम
आवाज़ आएगी न अब परवाज़ जाएगी।

कैंची से कोई आसमान काट रहा है।

now that we've split
literature, art—and—craft too
sound won't drift
nor will it soar—with scissors
someone is parting the sky

साथ ही साथ चला आया है, जितना भी सफ़र है
रास्ते पैरों में रस्सियों की तरह लिपटे हुए हैं

लौट के जाने से बल खुलते नहीं, और चढ़ेंगे।

have come along
as much as the journey was . . .
roads envelop legs like ropes
grip tightens on return
rather than loosening

सारी वादी उदास बैठी है,
मौसम-ए-गुल ने ख़ुदकुशी कर ली।

'माइन्ज़' पर पांव रख दिया उसने।

in despair
the whole valley crouches
as spring
pledged suicide
stepping on mines

नाप के वक़्त भरा जाता है, हर रेत-घड़ी में
इक तरफ़ ख़ाली हो जब फिर से उलट देते हैं उसको

उम्र जब ख़त्म हो, क्या मुझको वह उलटा नहीं सकता?

with a measurement
time is squeezed in each sandglass
as one side empties
it is upturned again—
when life ends can I be upturned?

चिड़ियाँ उड़ती हैं मेरे कांच के दरवाज़े के बाहर
नाचती धूप की चिंगारियों में जान भरी है

और मैं चिन्ता का तोदृह हूँ जो कमरे में पड़ा है।

outside my glass door
sparks of sunrays groove with zest
and birds fly—
        lying in the room
I'm   a mound of worry

यह आधा चाँद काले आसमाँ ऊपर
अंधेरा चाटती है, जीभ से जब रात,

कढ़ाई सुबह तक चट कर के जाती है!

this half-moon
above in the black sky
till morning
the night licks with its tongue
darkness from the wok

एक तम्बू लगा है सर्कस का
बाज़ीगर झूलते ही रहते हैं

ज़हन ख़ाली कभी नहीं होता

a tent
of a circus where
trapeze artists
always keep swinging—
the mind never stays idle

चलो ना शोर में बैठें, जहां कुछ न सुनाई दे
कि इस ख़ामोशी में तो सोच भी बजती है कानों में

बहुत बतियाया करती है यह फाफे कुटनी तनहाई!

let's sit in noise
where things remain unheard,
as in silence
thoughts too clank in ears—
this gossipy loneliness blabs

पत्थर की दीवार पे, लकड़ी के इक फ्रेम में, काँच के अन्दर फूल बने हैं
एक तसव्वुर खुशबू का और कितने सारे पहनावों में बन्द किया है

इश्क़ पे दिल का एक लिबास ही काफ़ी था, अब कितनी पोशाकें पहनेगा?

on the stone wall
flowers drawn inside a glass
are framed in wood . . .
sealed under countless layers
this fancy of fragrance

     of heart
     one attire was enough
     on love—
     how many costumes
     does it intend to wear

Acknowledgements

I am eternally grateful to Gulzar Sir for allowing me to translate his Triveni. His warmth and humbleness during the project really touched me. It was a dream-come-true moment, working with him, and one of those memories that will be cherished forever. The time spent with Gulzar Sir is poetry.

Thank you, Premanka Goswami, for helping me initiate the process. A sincere thanks to Chirag Thakkar, the editor of my book. Kudos to the team at Penguin and my wholehearted gratitude for offering my work a cosy home.

I would like to acknowledge the extraordinary debt that I owe Yaseen Anwer, who coined the idea of this book. His belief made this book a reality. It took him a year to persuade me that I could actually do this. I am much obliged as he took time to read and reread each version of every poem and rendered the role of a critic. I would not have been able to get my work done without his continual support and vision.

I am so thankful to all my haikai mentors, with whom I am exploring the universe of haikai literature, and my friend Samir Satam.

And loads of love to my family and my two little princesses, Sharanya and Ananya.

Scan QR code to access the
Penguin Random House India website